Y0-AGU-932

THE GHOST FILES

The World's Most

FAMOUS GHOSTS

by Joan Axelrod Contrada

Consultant:
Dr. Andrew Nichols
Director
American Institute of Parapsychology
Gainesville, Florida

CAPSTONE PRESS
a capstone imprint

Edge Books are published by Capstone Press,
151 Good Counsel Drive, P.O. Box 669, Mankato, Minnesota 56002.
www.capstonepub.com

 Books published by Capstone Press are manufactured with paper
containing at least 10 percent post-consumer waste.

Library of Congress Cataloging-in-Publication Data
Axelrod-Contrada, Joan.
    The world's most famous ghosts / by Joan Axelrod Contrada.
    p. cm.—(Edge Books. The Ghost Files)
Includes bibliographical references and index.
    Summary: "Describes reports of encounters with the ghosts of several
deceased entertainers and celebrities"—Provided by publisher.
    ISBN 978-1-4296-6516-2 (library binding)
    1. Ghosts—Juvenile literature. I. Title. II. Series.
BF1461.A97 2012
133.10973—dc22   2011003791

Editorial Credits
Aaron Sautter, editor; Tracy Davies, designer; Svetlana Zhurkin,
        media researcher; Eric Manske, production specialist

Photo Credits
Dreamstime: Steve Kingsman, 27 (bottom); Getty Images: Kevork Djansezian,
29, Time & Life Pictures/John Dominis, 23 (bottom), Washington Post/Bill
O'Leary, 9 (bottom); iStockphoto: Dwight Nadig, cover; Library of Congress,
9 (inset), 13, 21; Newscom: akg-images, 5, 25 (inset), Album, 27 (inset), Beitia
Archives, 23 (inset), MCT, 19, ZUMA Press/a13, 11 (bottom), ZUMA Press
Jonathan Alcorn, 25 (right), ZUMA Press/Toronto Star, 15, ZUMA Press
Toronto Star/Jeff Goode, 11 (inset); Shutterstock: Victorian Traditions, 7;
Wikimedia: Allan Warren, 17

Printed in the United States of America in Stevens Point, Wisconsin.
032011   006111WZF11

TABLE OF CONTENTS

CHAPTER 1

Stars Shine Bright After Death

Their spirits shimmer in the moonlight. They appear in glitzy nightclubs. They float like clouds through the places they enjoyed while alive. They're the stars of the spirit world—the ghosts of the rich and famous.

Apparitions of famous people cause a big stir wherever they are seen. Reporters show up. Ghost hunters are called in, and TV cameras roll. Could the souls of our brightest stars be hanging around for one last curtain call? Or are we the ones who can't let go? Nobody knows if ghosts are real or not. But it's always a thrill to hear about celebrities—even if they're in ghostly form.

apparition – the visible appearance of a ghost

FACT

The ghost of silent-screen star Rudolph Valentino is one of the most reported spirits in Hollywood. The "Latin Lover" died at the age of 31 from complications of an ulcer.

CHAPTER 2

U.S. PRESIDENTS

The president of the United States is one of the most powerful people in the world. With one stroke of the pen, the president can change the course of history. According to some reports, a few of the country's most beloved presidents' spirits still live among us.

GEORGE WASHINGTON

The roar of muskets and cannon fire fills the air on July 2, 1863. It's the height of the Civil War (1861–1865). Union soldiers are holding Little Round Top hill near Gettysburg, Pennsylvania. They are nearly out of ammunition and hope. As they reload their muskets, a ghostly figure suddenly appears on a white horse. The figure commands them to charge down the hill.

"Fix bayonets! Charge!" he orders, leading them to victory. According to legend, the mysterious man was the ghost of President George Washington. Soldiers reported that he was dressed in his uniform from the Revolutionary War (1775–1783).

Washington died of a throat infection in 1799. However, his spirit may have returned to help guide the nation through its most troubled times. The misty form on horseback is said to still haunt the countryside near Gettysburg.

GEORGE WASHINGTON

Abraham Lincoln

Late at night, the tall `specter` of President Abraham Lincoln drifts through the White House. He raps on doors. He peers sadly out windows. And he hangs around the Lincoln bedroom. At least, that's what numerous witnesses have reported.

In 1945 Queen Wilhelmina of the Netherlands came to visit the White House. She stayed in the Lincoln bedroom. Late at night, she heard something rapping on her door. She opened the door and gasped. There stood the figure of Abe Lincoln dressed in his famous coat and top hat. Shocked by the sight, she fainted. The apparition was gone when she awoke.

Several years later, President Lyndon Johnson's wife said she felt Lincoln's presence. She mentioned feeling a strange coldness and sense of unease. Even President Ronald Reagan's dog refused to go into the Lincoln bedroom. Whenever he got near the room, he'd start barking and growling, and then back away.

`specter - a ghost`

Does Lincoln's ghost wander the halls of the White House? No one can say. But something unexplained seems to be happening in the former president's old room.

ABRAHAM LINCOLN

Several visitors have reported feeling a ghostly presence in the Lincoln bedroom.

CHAPTER 3

OUTLAWS AND GANGSTERS

A getaway car squeals. Shots ring out, and another criminal is killed in a gang shootout. But who's to say he won't return as a ghost? After all, outlaws and gangsters live by their own rules.

AL CAPONE

Visitors to Al Capone's grave in Hillside, Illinois, sometimes report feeling like they're being watched. They say a ghostly presence watches over the final resting place of the famous gangster. They feel that they need to show proper respect for the legendary crime boss—or else.

FACT Al Capone's ghost is said to also haunt the prison at Alcatraz Island in San Francisco, California. During the 1930s, he played banjo with the prison band. Visitors to Alcatraz have reported hearing eerie banjo music coming from Capone's old prison cell.

During the 1920s Capone challenged anyone who got in his way. He ruled an empire of criminals and their illegal activities. The cigar-smoking gangster died in 1947.

Since then, many visitors have placed cigars or bottles of alcohol at the gangster's grave. Perhaps they're simply remembering a former time. Or maybe they're truly afraid that Capone's ghost will come back to haunt the living.

AL CAPONE

ALPHONSE CAPONE
1899 ——— 1947
MY JESUS MERCY

Some people think Capone's ghost haunts his gravesite.

JESSE JAMES

Spurs jangle on cowboy boots as an eerie figure takes shape. The ghost drifts in and out of rooms at the St. James Hotel in Selma, Alabama. Guests swear it's the ghost of famous outlaw Jesse James. Jesse liked to vacation at the St. James with his girlfriend, Lucinda, and his dog in the mid-1800s.

It seems that the couple's ghosts like to return to their favorite vacation spot. Guests say they've seen Lucinda's tall, dark-haired figure drifting through room 214. Her spirit is known for wearing lavender-scented perfume. Jesse's dog is also rumored to romp around on the hotel's second floor. Nobody has ever seen the dog. However, several people have reported hearing it barking.

FACT From 1993 to 1997, pop star Madonna lived in a mansion reportedly haunted by the gangster Bugsy Siegel. Madonna once told a friend that she felt an unsafe presence in the house.

Downstairs, witnesses have reported seeing Jesse's lifelike image dressed in old cowboy duds. His ghost often hovers over his favorite table to the left of the bar. Sometimes people say that glasses on the bar rattle for no reason. When hotel employees yell at the ghost to stop his mischief, the glasses stop rattling.

JESSE JAMES

CHAPTER 4

ENTERTAINERS

Some people seem born to be entertainers. They know how to capture an audience's attention. According to some reports, a few stars of the stage keep capturing people's attention even after death.

HARRY HOUDINI

Magician Harry Houdini was a master at escaping from chains, handcuffs, and straightjackets. But when he died on October 31, 1926, did Houdini escape from the ultimate trap? Did he manage to return from death itself?

Some people claim the Great Houdini did just that. During one show performed in his honor, witnesses say they felt cold spots in the auditorium. They think Houdini's ghost stopped by to see if the tricks were being performed properly.

FACT Each year on Halloween, the Houdini Museum hosts an online séance. Fans are encouraged to try to contact the magician's spirit. They can send their results—or lack of them—to the museum.

Other people claim they've seen Houdini's ghost at the remains of his old home in Laurel Canyon, California. The house burned down in 1959. Some witnesses claim they've seen a dark figure standing silently on the stone staircases that led up to the house. Others have reported seeing someone wandering through the gardens. The identity of the spooky figure remains a mystery.

Houdini was a master escape artist. Did his spirit manage to escape death?

LIBERACE

One night, a strange thing happens at Carluccio's restaurant in Las Vegas, Nevada. Glasses rattle and the lights go out. Suddenly someone remembers it's Liberace's birthday. The legendary pianist, who once owned the restaurant, died in 1987. The employees quickly wish Liberace a happy birthday—and the lights flicker back on.

Since Liberace died, Carluccio's staff workers have reported numerous encounters with his ghost. On one occasion, an employee was cleaning the mirrors in the piano room. He reported seeing Liberace's spirit appear dressed in a sparkling cape.

Ghostly activity at Carluccio's supposedly peaks on Liberace's birthday and the anniversary of his death. The air turns cold. Toilets flush by themselves, and strange noises are heard. One employee claimed she once told an unflattering joke about Liberace. Seconds later, a wine bottle crashed to the floor by her feet. Was the ghost trying to get back at her? Or did the bottle just fall by accident? Nobody knows for certain.

FACT Liberace's sparkling costumes inspired other stars, such as Elvis Presley and Michael Jackson, to wear glitzy outfits too.

CHAPTER 5

WRITERS

Sometimes authors live very private lives. From a distance, these solitary writers seem to live within the mysterious worlds they create. Perhaps that's why some people believe they've returned from the dead as ghosts.

EDITH WHARTON

Edith Wharton's former home in western Massachusetts was called The Mount. Visitors to The Mount have reported hearing floors creaking and doors slamming. A mysterious laugh has also been heard. People often recoil in fear. Perhaps they sense the unfriendly energy left from Wharton's stay from 1903 to 1911. During this time, her marriage to husband Teddy was crumbling. It's also when she wrote her emotionally haunting books and ghost stories.

Some visitors have reported feeling Teddy's ghost holding them down in their sleep. Others claim to have seen a ghostly woman reading in Edith's old bedroom. The spirit was said to resemble the famous author. Yet another visitor claimed to see the shadow of a man in old-fashioned clothes. He appeared to be Edith's secret lover. Recently, investigators from the TV show *Ghost Hunters* visited The Mount. They recorded the sounds of footsteps and disembodied voices. None of the evidence they found could be explained logically. Perhaps supernatural forces really do exist.

Edith Wharton's troubled spirit is said to still wander the halls of her old home.

Edgar Allan Poe

Under the starlit winter sky, a dark figure visits Edgar Allan Poe's gravesite in Baltimore, Maryland. He's been showing up for more than 50 years. The shadowy figure appears only in the wee hours of January 19th, which is Poe's birthday. He carefully places a bottle of wine and three roses on Poe's grave. Then, like a character from one of Poe's eerie stories, he disappears into the night.

Before his death in 1849, Poe led a life of poverty, illness, and heartbreak. Both of his parents died within three years of his birth. His wife died just a few years after they were married. The heartbroken author soon sank into despair.

FACT Some visitors to the Edgar Allan Poe Museum in Shreveport, Louisiana, have reported seeing the author's ghost. But no one has been able to identify him clearly. Perhaps in death, as in life, the author likes to protect his privacy.

Since Poe's death, there have been several reports of ghostly activity at his former home. Windows fly open by themselves. People have heard mysterious voices. Strange lights have been seen when the house was known to be empty. Does Poe's spirit remain in this world, unable to let go of his grief? Could the mysterious figure seen by Poe's grave really be the author's ghost? The answer may never be known.

Edgar Allan Poe's creepy stories often reflected the tragedy of his own life.

CHAPTER 6

MOVIE STARS

Lights—camera—action! Sometimes, the ghosts of famous actors and actresses are reported far from the silver screen. Maybe they want to live in the spotlight forever. Or perhaps fans just like to remember their favorite stars.

JOHN WAYNE

Not far from Hollywood, a gust of air ruffles the stillness at sea. Beer glasses clang at the bar on a private yacht. Then a smoky apparition appears by the bedroom door, wearing a cowboy hat. The figure slips away and vanishes into the night.

Several visitors have claimed to see the ghost of the yacht's previous owner, famous movie star John Wayne. The legendary actor starred in many Western films. He often liked to relax aboard his private yacht called the *Wild Goose*.

yacht – a large boat used for sailing or racing

Two months before his death in 1979, the actor sold the *Wild Goose*. Today the boat's owners use it for dinner cruises. One guest claimed to have seen John Wayne's ghost dressed in his old ship captain's cap.

Some ghosts seem trapped in the sorrows they suffered in life. But John Wayne's spirit appears to be happy to return to his favorite place to relax.

JOHN WAYNE

According to reports, John Wayne's ghost seems to enjoy visiting the Wild Goose.

Marilyn Monroe

A misty form drifts through Marilyn Monroe's old bedroom at her former home in Brentwood, California. Ghost hunters stop dead in their tracks. This is the exact spot where the glamorous star died.

Many people believe that Monroe took sleeping pills to kill herself on August 4, 1962. However, several psychics claim she took the pills simply to battle insomnia. She never meant to die.

Some visitors to the Hollywood Roosevelt hotel have also claimed to see Monroe's ghost. The glamorous movie star often stayed at the famous hotel. The hotel lobby now holds the mirror that once stood in Monroe's favorite room. Witnesses have reported seeing the star's reflection primping herself in the mirror. Others have reported seeing Monroe's ghost lounging by the pool. Still others say they've glimpsed her misty image in the ladies' restroom. Like other reported spirits, Monroe's ghost seems to enjoy staying in a familiar location.

psychic — someone who claims to communicate with the dead

HOTEL
ROOSEVELT

MARILYN MONROE

The spirit of actor Montgomery Clift is also
said to haunt the Hollywood Roosevelt hotel.

insomnia — when someone has difficulty sleeping

CHAPTER 7

MUSICIANS

Live hard, have fun, and die young. Those words seem to define many music stars. But sometimes they seem to keep rocking even after death. Fans of famous singers believe strange events might prove their heroes are still around—in ghostly form.

ELVIS PRESLEY

Ladders fall. Lightbulbs blow out. And eerie noises are heard in an old recording studio in Nashville, Tennessee. It's the same studio where Elvis Presley recorded his 1956 hit "Heartbreak Hotel." Some visitors believe the studio is haunted by Elvis' spirit.

FACT A psychic once claimed Elvis' ghost confessed his unhappiness to her. She says he was especially upset about the large number of Elvis imitators.

Elvis Presley died on August 16, 1977. He was at his famous mansion called Graceland in Memphis, Tennessee. But it would seem that the "King of Rock 'n' Roll" is hesitant to leave his fans behind.

At the Hilton Hotel in Las Vegas, Nevada, witnesses claim they've seen Elvis' ghost wearing his famous white jumpsuit. His ghost is also said to roam from room to room at Graceland. Some visitors even claim they've seen him in the Graceland Chapel. He was reportedly marrying another famous ghost—movie star Marilyn Monroe.

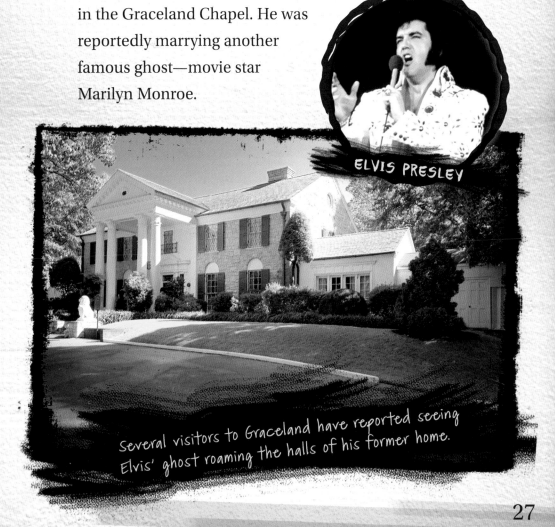

ELVIS PRESLEY

Several visitors to Graceland have reported seeing Elvis' ghost roaming the halls of his former home.

MICHAEL JACKSON

It's a sad day at Neverland Ranch in Santa Barbara, California. Michael Jackson, the "King of Pop," has just died. Famous talk show host Larry King is taping his TV show at Neverland. King interviews family members while his film crew tours Jackson's home. Later, when the show airs on the Internet, a shadowy figure is seen in the background in one brief shot.

Fans debate Jackson's supposed ghost in this shot. Believers say they can see Jackson's image in the shadow. One witness insists the figure has Jackson's hair style. Another claims the shadow has Jackson's distinctive walk. However, others argue that it's just the shadow of a TV crew person.

After Jackson's death in 2009, a memorial service was held at the Staples Center in Los Angeles, California. Several fans claim Jackson's ghost appeared at the service. Are the sightings proof that Jackson's spirit exists? Most people feel it's just wishful thinking. They believe devoted fans are simply hanging on to memories of their favorite star, longing to see him again.

Many fans believe they saw Michael Jackson's ghost at his memorial service in 2009.

UNSOLVABLE MYSTERY

Throughout history, many mysteries have been solved. Long ago, people believed the world was flat. We now know it's round. However, many mysterious things in the world remain unexplained. It's impossible to know if ghosts exist. But one thing is certain—celebrities live long after death through their words, movies, and music.

GLOSSARY

apparition (ap-uh-RISH-uhn)—the visible appearance of a ghost or spirit

haunt (HAWNT)—to cause unexplained events to occur or appear as a ghost in a certain place

insomnia (in-SOM-nee-uh)—not being able to fall asleep or stay asleep

psychic (SYE-kik)—a person who claims to sense, see, or hear things that others do not; some psychics say they can sense and communicate with ghosts

séance (SEY-ahns)—a meeting to contact the spirits of the dead

specter (SPEK-tur)—a ghost

spirit (SPIHR-it)—the soul or invisible part of a person believed to control thoughts and feelings; some people believe the spirit leaves the body after death

straightjacket (strayt-JAK-it)—a garment made of strong material designed to bind the arms of a violent or disoriented person

yacht (YAHT)—a large boat used for sailing or racing

READ MORE

Axelrod-Contrada, Joan. *Ghoulish Ghost Stories.*
Scary Stories. Mankato, Minn.: Capstone Press, 2011.

Nobleman, Marc Tyler. *Ghosts.* Atomic. Chicago:
Raintree, 2007.

Whiting, Jim. *Scary Stories.* Really Scary Stuff.
Mankato, Minn.: Capstone Press, 2010.

INTERNET SITES

FactHound offers a safe, fun way to find Internet sites
related to this book. All of the sites on FactHound have
been researched by our staff.

Here's all you do:

Visit *www.facthound.com*

Type in this code: 9781429665162

Check out projects, games and lots more at
www.capstonekids.com

INDEX